My First Story of the First EASTER

Retold by Deanna Draper Buck

Illustrated by Jerry Harston

This book belongs to

Presented by

Date

My First
Story of the First
EASTER

Retold by Deanna Draper Buck

Illustrated by Jerry Harston

DESERET
BOOK

SALT LAKE CITY, UTAH

First printing as board book 2008.
First printing in paperbound 2013.

Library of Congress Cataloging-in-Publication Data

Buck, Deanna Draper. My first story of the first Easter / Deanna Draper Buck.
  p. cm.
ISBN 978-1-59038-871-6 (board book : alk. paper)
ISBN 978-1-60907-527-9 (paperbound)
1. Jesus Christ—Mormon interpretations—Juvenile literature.
2. Easter—Juvenile literature. 3. Board books. I. Title.
BX8643.J4B83 2008
232.9'7—dc22   2007041135

Printed in Mexico
R. R. Donnelley, Reynosa, Mexico

10 9 8 7 6 5 4 3 2

For George—DB
For My Grandchildren—JH

JESUS TEACHES THE PEOPLE

For three years Jesus had been teaching the people to love Heavenly Father and to be kind and to help each other. He healed the sick and made the blind to see, the lame to walk, and the deaf to hear. Some who had died were even brought back to life by Him.

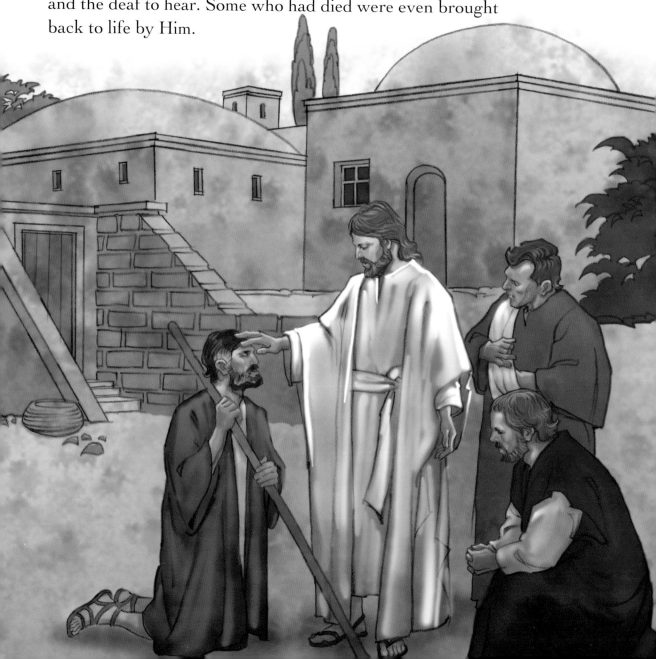

Jesus had also chosen twelve men, called apostles, to
work with Him and to be witnesses of His miracles.
He taught that the greatest love we can have is to be
willing to die for a friend and that He was preparing
to die for the sins of the world.

JESUS' TRIUMPHAL ENTRY INTO JERUSALEM

When the time came for Jesus to finish his mortal mission, He traveled to Jerusalem and rode into the great city on a donkey. It was the time of a special celebration called the feast of the Passover, and many people were in Jerusalem for the feast.

When Jesus entered the city, the people ran to greet Him. Those who loved Him and believed He was the Son of God waved palm branches and shouted, "Hosanna! Hosanna!" They were happy to see Jesus and eager to hear more of His teachings.

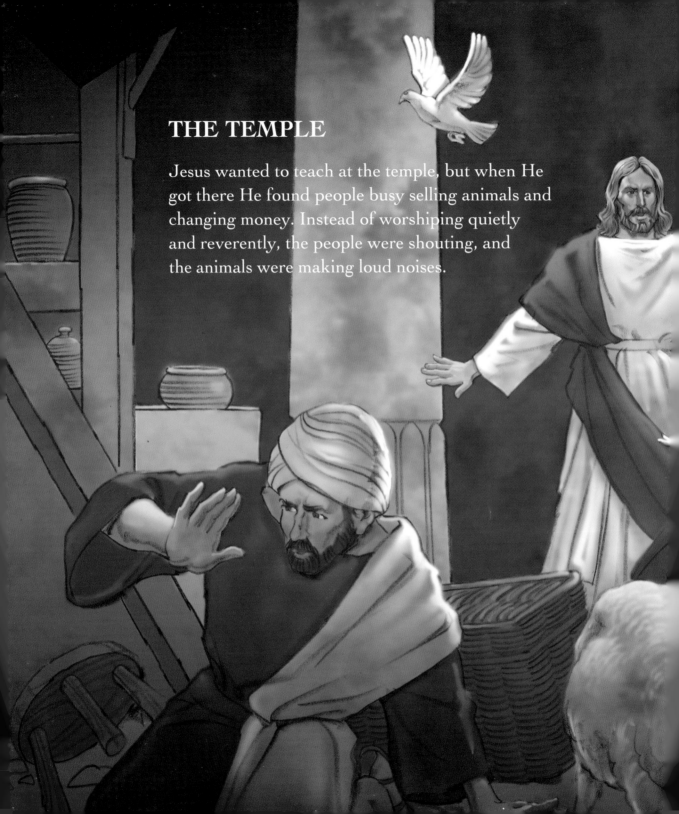

THE TEMPLE

Jesus wanted to teach at the temple, but when He got there He found people busy selling animals and changing money. Instead of worshiping quietly and reverently, the people were shouting, and the animals were making loud noises.

The confusion made Jesus sad, and He told the greedy men to take their animals and leave the temple. Then Jesus said to the people: "My house shall be called the house of prayer; but ye have made it a den of thieves."

TEACHING AT THE TEMPLE

Many people were at the temple and wanted to hear Jesus teach. The wicked rulers did not believe Jesus was the Son of God. They were jealous of Him and wanted to kill Jesus, but they were afraid to do so because the people loved Jesus. Judas, one of Jesus' apostles, told the wicked men he would help them capture Jesus. The wicked men paid Judas thirty pieces of silver for his evil work.

THE LAST SUPPER

Jesus and His apostles met together in an upper room for the feast of the Passover. Jesus blessed some bread and wine and gave it to His apostles. He told them to remember His body and His blood whenever they ate the bread and drank the wine.

Jesus also knelt on the floor and washed the feet of the apostles. He was teaching them to serve each other. He said to them, "I give you a new commandment, As I have loved you, love one another."

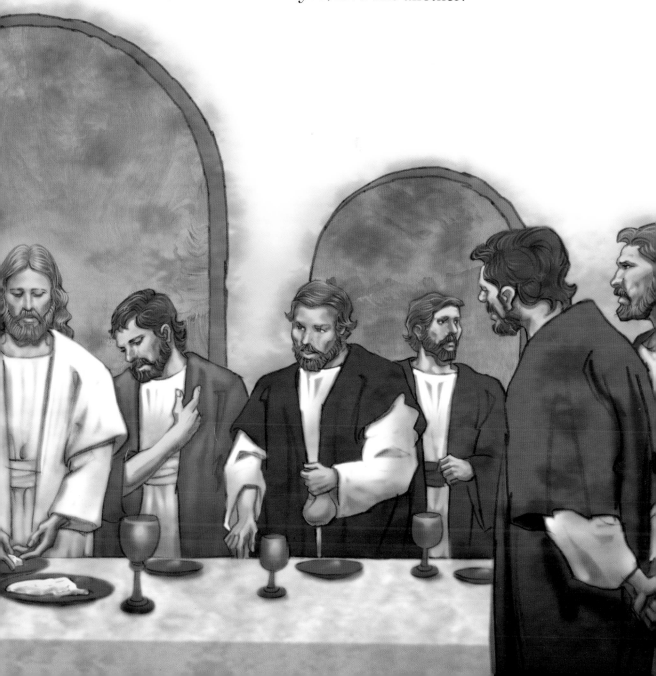

THE GARDEN OF GETHSEMANE

Judas left the Last Supper early so he could go tell the men who hated Jesus where to find Him. After the feast, Jesus and the rest of the apostles went into a garden called Gethsemane.

Jesus asked the apostles to wait for Him and to pray. Then He went a little farther into the garden to be alone. He prayed to Heavenly Father and suffered for our sins. This "atonement" made it possible for us to be forgiven when we repent so that we can return to live with Heavenly Father after we die.

JUDAS

Judas led Jesus' enemies to the Garden of Gethsemane. There, he kissed Jesus on the cheek so the wicked men would know which man was Jesus. When Peter saw that they were going to capture Jesus, he used his sword and cut off the ear of one of the wicked men, but Jesus quickly replaced the ear and healed the wound. Jesus loves everyone, even His enemies.

HEROD AND PILATE

The wicked men took Jesus to the Roman rulers Herod and Pilate. They told lies about Jesus, but Herod and Pilate didn't believe the lies and wanted to let Jesus go free. The wicked men shouted more and told more lies. Pilate wasn't very brave, and he didn't want the angry people to cause a lot of trouble, so he finally told them they could crucify Jesus.

THE CRUCIFIXION

Roman soldiers took Jesus and nailed Him to a wooden cross and crucified Him between two thieves. While hanging on the cross, Jesus told His apostle John to take care of His mother, Mary. He also asked Heavenly Father to forgive the men who crucified Him. Jesus was always kind and concerned about others, even while He was in great pain.

BURIAL

After Jesus died on the cross, His friends took His body and laid it in a tomb. The wicked men remembered Jesus had said He would be resurrected in three days. They didn't believe He would come alive again, but they didn't want Jesus' friends to take the body away and pretend He had risen from the dead. His enemies had a large stone rolled in front of the tomb to block the door, and they had Roman soldiers guard the tomb.

THE RESURRECTION

On the Sunday morning after Jesus was crucified, some kind women went to the tomb. They wanted to prepare Jesus' body for burial, but when they got there, they found the stone had been rolled away from the door, and the Roman soldiers were gone! When the women looked inside the tomb, they saw that Jesus' body was gone also! An angel told the women that Jesus had been resurrected. The angel told them to go and tell the apostles the wonderful news that Jesus was alive again.

JESUS VISITS HIS APOSTLES

Soon the resurrected Jesus appeared to the apostles. They were joyful to see Him again. Jesus had them touch the nail marks in His hands and feet, they ate food together, and He taught them the things they needed to know to lead His church. He also told them He needed to go back to heaven but that He would send the Holy Ghost to guide them. The Holy Ghost would also help and comfort them. Jesus told His apostles to go and teach people everywhere about Heavenly Father, to be kind and to help each other, to keep the commandments, and to be baptized.

JESUS VISITS THE NEPHITES

Before Jesus was crucified, He told the people in Jerusalem that He had other sheep He needed to visit. The people living in America were His other sheep. The people in America knew Jesus had been born and were waiting for Him to visit them. When Jesus was crucified, there were storms and earthquakes in America, and it was totally dark for three days.

After His resurrection, Jesus appeared to the Nephites at the temple in the land of Bountiful. The people in America were happy when Jesus came to visit them. He taught them His gospel and blessed their little children. His visit was so wonderful that after He left, the people in America lived in peace and love for two hundred years.

WHY WE CELEBRATE EASTER

Easter is the time each year when we remember that Jesus was resurrected. His spirit came back into his dead body, and He came alive again. He was now glorified and went to live with his Father in Heaven.

The good news is that because of Jesus, even though we will all die, each of us will also be resurrected, or come alive again. Then, if we have been obedient and kept His commandments, Heavenly Father will forgive our sins and let us live forever with Him and with our families and friends in heaven. There can be no greater blessing. And that is why Easter is so important.

About the Author

Award-winning, bestselling author Deanna Draper Buck and her husband have been married over forty years. They currently live in Hooper, Utah, where they enjoy gardening, the Great Salt Lake, and entertaining their nineteen grandchildren. Deanna has written nine LDS children's books, explaining gospel principles, Church history, and scriptures stories in a simplified style.

About the Illustrator

Jerry Harston held a degree in graphic design and illustrated more than thirty children's books. He received many honors for his art, and his clients included numerous Fortune 500 corporations. Jerry passed away in December 2009.